WILD WEST™ DIVERSITY

Sharing the rarely and untold stories of multicultural contributions to the settling of the American Wild West.

Dedication

To every little boy and little girl that dreamed of being a cowboy or cowgirl this book is for you.

To Western enthusiasts all over the world keep the celebration and the contributions going so future generations can connect to their heritage and learn to build harmony across our communities.

Wild West Diversity Livestream, Podcast and eNewsletter
follow us on your favorite social media platform

@WildWestDiversity

SUBSCRIBE TO OUR YOUTUBE CHANNEL
AT WILD WEST DIVERSITY TO WATCH AND HEAR
INTERVIEWS WITH LIVING LEGENDS
OR WATCH LIVE EVERY THURSDAY AT 5 PM CST
ON LINKEDIN, FACEBOOK OR YOUTUBE.

TO ENJOY OUR WEEKLY ENEWSLETTER VISIT & SUBSCRIBE AT
WWW.WILDWESTDIVERSITY.COM

Introduction

The adventurous saga of the American West is filled with tales of Indians, military actions, missionaries, mountain men, gamblers, pioneers, cowboys, cowgirls, outlaws, lawmen, horse trainers, musicians and more. In the vast lands west of the Mississippi River, they traveled the plains, conquered the mountains, built large ranches and forged towns in beautiful and desolate places.

After the Civil War, many went West seeking a less hostile environment and a peaceful place to raise their families. What they found, in many cases, was a different kind of hostile environment. It was hard, back-breaking work to farm, ranch and build communities where none had existed before. Economic, political and social challenges existed that had not been encountered before.

The dangers of terrain, rivers, forests, deserts, weather, bandits, and war parties were a different type of challenge for African American adventurers.

As the American West grew and evolved people from various walks of life continued to make their mark on the collective history of all Americans. The people in this book attest to the fact that courage, determination and a dream can carry you to a new place.

The historical heroes and heroines in these pages chose a different way of life and each have a story to tell. They lived on their own terms, creating lives out of nothing and leaving a proud legacy for future generations.

Now young and old alike can read and hear the other facts of a wild, diverse and never dull account of both African American men and women who followed their individual dreams and ideas.

Liz Lawless
Crazy L Ranch

Elizabeth "Liz" Ann Lawless is the author of 12 Books including *Western Legends: Yesterday & Today ... African Americans 1798 to 2009* which this book is based on. If you want to read the full stories please get your copy at Amazon or other retail outlets. She has taken the stories and historical characters of the past who lived these wild and adventurous lives and created a children's version with the help of her talented illustrator Hatice Bayramoglu.

She knows children of all ages and adults young at heart will enjoy these stories of ordinary people who lived extraordinary lives because of their choices and actions. All of them are great role models for today.

Liz and Hatice hope you enjoy these stories and illustrations. This is only the first book in the Western Legends Kids Series so we hope you will keep watch for new books in the future. The next will be *African American Living Legends: Today* where readers will meet real people keeping the Western Legacy alive for future generations. There also are companion coloring books.

Don't forget to follow us or subscribe to our social media channels or join our VIP Club to get early notice of our upcoming new books, speaking engagements, book signings and other virtual and live events.

If you have a group you would like Liz to speak to please contact her at wildwestdiversity@gmail.com to schedule a time to discuss budgets and opportunities.

James Pierson Beckwourth (1798-1866)
Trapper, Trader & Army Scout

As a teenager James joined his first fur trapping company as a Wranger and went on his first expedition of the Rocky Mountains. As a grown man, he discovered the lowest mountain pass through the Sierra Nevada Mountains. Known as Beckwourth Trail, this road allowed travelers to reach California while avoiding the harsh winters of the Northern routes.

"Never recognized at the time the people living in the area now renamed their largest park Beckwourth Riverfront Park."

Famous trapper, Indian fighter, trader and army scout

Henrietta Williams Foster (1822-1926) Went on Cattle Drives and Owned Property

Known as Aunt Rittie, she was a rare person in her time, a woman who worked cattle with men and went on many cattle drives. She had no formal education but she was smart and gained skill with herbal remedies as a midwife and taught others. She married Charles Foster and bought a place in Refugio for twenty-five dollars by paying it out a quarter a week, another rarity among women. When she thought her neighbor was trying to steal her land she hit him in the head with a hammer. She went and confessed to the sheriff and when they returned to her property they found the neighbor was not dead. She told the sheriff "arrest that man."

Courageous midwife and property owner

Stagecoach Mary Fields (1832-1914)
First African American Woman to Delivery Mail in Wyoming

Mary stood 6-foot and weighed 200-pounds. She was a cigar-smoking, gun-toting pioneer who settled her arguments with her fists, and once in a while with her six-shooter. She also played cards and drank whiskey at the local saloon. Her childhood friend, Mother Amadeus, asked the government to give Mary a mail route, but she had to win it first by hooking up a team of horses faster than anyone else. So she did. She held this job for eight years, never missing a day regardless of bad terrain, wild animals, bandits or freezing temperatures, and that's when she became known as STAGECOACH MARY.

Stagecoach Mary card shark, fighter, mail woman

Bass Reeves (1838-1910)
United States Deputy Marshal

Bass Reeves was the first Black United States Deputy Marshal west of the Mississippi River. He possessed a superior knowledge of Native languages, the people, towns and Indian territory. It was immediately known that he was not one of the ruthless White outlaws who had plagued law abiding citizens, stagecoaches, trains and settlers. He often wore disguises (once dressed as a woman) and worked with an Indian partner. Although he could not read and write, he arrested over 3,000 felons and killed fourteen outlaws in gun battles; never being shot or wounded himself.

Bass Reeves lawman and master of disguises

Cathay Williams / William Cathay (1842-1924)
38th U.S. Infantry Buffalo Soldiers
Only Documented Female Buffalo Soldier

An independent young woman, Cathay Williams wanted to make her own way after the Civil War. Before 1948, it was illegal for women to serve in the military, so on November 15, 1866, at age 22, William Cathay was officially enlisted as a Buffalo Soldier. His height was measured at 5 foot 9 inches, too tall to join the cavalry, so he (she) was assigned to the 38th Infantry Regiment in New Mexico. Cathay served two years before a doctor discovered her secret and she was immediately given a medical discharge and told to go to a distant town so no one would know she served in the Army.

Cathay Williams only female Buffalo Soldier

Bois Ikard (1844-1929)
Trail Driver and Cattleman

As a teenager, Ikard learn the dangers of Indian raids and cowboy skills of riding and roping. After serving in the Union Army, he hired out his skills and service as a trail driver to Oliver Loving. After Loving was killed fighting Comanches in New Mexico, Ikard continued working with Charles Goodnight often carrying the money and reporting back when thieves wanted to steal their cattle. As a black cowboy he was never considered a threat. They became lifelong friends.

"Bose Ikard served with me for four years on the Goodnight-Loving Trail, never shirked a duty or disobeyed and order, rode in many stampedes, fought Comanches three times – splendid behavior," said Charles Goodnight.

Bois Ikard trail driver, banker, detective, and loyal friend

Emmanuel Stance (1847-1887)
First Buffalo Soldier to Win the Medal of Honor During the Indian Wars

Emmanuel Stance was a bright-eyed, stubborn, intelligent well-spoken man only 5 feet tall. Despite his height, Stance's ability to read and write eventually persuaded the Army recruiter to enlist him. Stance became a member of Company F, 9th U.S. Cavalry. Stance was promoted to corporal then sergeant serving at San Antonio, Fort Davis and Fort McKavett. The Buffalo Soldiers were besieged by 16 Indian attacks but manage to keep the Forts and people inside safe.

Emmanuel Stance fierce Indian fighter and protector

Johanna July (1850-1930)
Trained Horses for the Military & Ranchers

Johanna was a tall, barefoot girl who wore bright homemade dresses, gold earrings and necklaces. She developed her own method of taming horses. Leading them into the Rio Grande, she grabbed their mane and with just a rope around their neck and rode bareback. The horses nervous in the river and tired from swimming, soon lost the strength to buck. When her father died and her brother left home, she continued to tame wild horses and work stock for the U.S. Army and area ranchers. It was one of the few ways she could earn a living.

Johanna July horse trainer and stock woman

Nat Love (1854-1921)
Deadwood Dick Sharpshooting Cowboy

After the Civil War, Love heard of the opportunities out West for cowhands. He traveled to Dodge City, Kansas, working for two different ranches where he honed his roping and marksmanship skills. In 1876, he entered the Deadwood, South Dakota Rodeo on July 4th where he won the rope, throw, tie, bridle, saddle and bronco riding contests. Love also impressed onlookers with his shooting skills. He won $200.00 for hitting the target 14 times compared to the 8 by other contestants. This kind of skill and money guaranteed a black cowboy equal treatment in town or on the trail.

"I gloried in the danger, and the wild and free life of the plains, the new country I was continually traversing, and the many new scenes and incidents continually arising in the life of a Rough Rider."

Nat Love well-known cowboy and sharpshooter

24

Second Lieutenant Henry O. Flipper (1856-1940)
First African American to Graduate from West Point

Henry Ossian Flipper's dream was to become a military officer. Georgia congressman James Freeman sent his nomination to the Secretary of War. After passing the required tests, Flipper officially entered the academy on July 1, 1873. The young cadet did well at French, Spanish, engineering and law. In 1877, he was the first black to graduate from West Point. A Second Lieutenant, he was assigned to the 10th Cavalry on the frontier at Fort Sill in Indian Territory. While at Fort Sill, Flipper used his engineering skills to construct a new drainage system *"Flipper's Ditch"* to help eliminate stagnate ponds and cases of malaria. After the Army, he took his skills and become a respected surveyor. In 1890, he opened his own engineering and mining office in Arizona.

Henry O. Flipper, officer, surveyor and engineer

Corporal Isaiah Mays (1858-1925)
24th US Infantry Buffalo Soldier - Medal of Honor

Isaiah Mays joined the Army from Columbus Barracks, Ohio and was assigned to Company B of the 24th U.S. Infantry Regiment of the Buffalo Soldiers under the direction of Major Joseph Washington Wham. Corporal Mays was awarded the Medal of Honor in 1890 for *"gallantry and meritorious conduct"* while defending an Army pay wagon against masked bandits near Tucson, Arizona. Mays, shot in both legs, walked and crawled two miles to a nearby ranch to sound the alarm. The robbers got away with $29,000 in gold (worth nearly half a million dollars today). In 2001, Mays finally received a Medal of Honor headstone from the U.S. Department of Veterans Affairs for his bravery 110 years earlier.

Isaiah Mays soldier and medal of honor recipient

Sergeant Benjamin Brown (1859-1910)
24th US Infantry Buffalo Soldier - Medal of Honor

Benjamin Brown entered military service at Harrisburg, Pennsylvania. He was stationed with Company C, 24th U.S. Infantry at Fort Grant. He was a part of the same infantry as Corporal Isaiah Mays. With a cry of *"Look out!"* a buckskin-clad bandit and his gang opened fire on the wagon train from an advantageous position on the bluff. The soldiers grabbed their guns and those that could took cover to return fire. Brown and some others were struck quickly by the hail of bullets. Major Wham stated that *"Sergeant Brown, made his entire fight from open ground."* Brown's Medal of Honor citation reads in part that *"although shot in the abdomen...did not leave the field until again wounded through both arms."* The money was never found, although suspects were brought to trial.

Benjamin Brown courageous soldier and fighter

Matthew "Bones Hooks (1867-1951)
Top Horse Trainer

Matthew "Bones" Hooks gained the nickname "Bones" because he was so thin. From age nine until adulthood he drove a chuck wagon and worked as a ranch hand for a number of ranches in West Texas. He went on many trail drives, raised horses with a White partner and became a top horse breaker. Cowboys kept bringing him wild horses as a challenge, until they realized there was none he couldn't ride. In his later years, Hooks participated in several pioneer, cowboy and historical gatherings recounting his cowboy memories of the Old West.

Hooks was the first African American to join the Western Cowpunchers Association of Amarillo and the Western Cowboys Association of Montana. He also was the first Black man to serve on a Potter County Grand Jury.

Matthew "Bones" Hooks outstanding ranch hand and horse trainer

William "Bill" Pickett (1870-1932)
"The Dusky Demon" Super Cowhand

Legendary cowboy William "Bill" Pickett was of black and Indian descent. Pickett signed on with the famous Oklahoma 101 Ranch Show in 1905. With his horse, Spradley, he performed across the U.S., Canada, Mexico, South America and England. Known as *"The Dusky Demon"* Pickett gave exhibitions in Texas and throughout the west. His performance at the Cheyenne Frontier Days (America's best-known rodeo) was spectacular. He often identified himself as Indian in order to perform, since blacks were banned from competing in rodeos. He became the first black cowboy movie star when he performed in Richard E. Norman's movie *"The Bull-Dogger"*. Pickett was the first African-American to be inducted into the National Western Heritage and Cowboy Museum Hall of Fame in Oklahoma City.

Bill Pickett invented rodeo event Bulldoggin' or Steer Wrestling

Jesse Stahl (1879-1938)
Suicide & Bronc Rider

Born in Tennessee in 1883, Jesse and his brother Ambrose began competing in Rodeos 1901. Stahl started with steers and bulls where he won several competitions, but it was when he and another black cowboy, Ty Stokes, rode a bucking horse back to back in what was called "a suicide ride" that he found his true event. Considered one of the greatest bronc riders ever, he never was awarded the top prizes because he was Black. Stahl never failed to out-ride and out-show his competition. In one particular instance, he placed second when he should have won. In a daring and deliberate move, he rode out backwards – on "Glass Eye" a wild bucking horse that had never been ridden! In 1979, he was the second African American inducted into the National Western Heritage and Cowboy Museum Hall of Fame in Oklahoma City.

Jesse Stahl greatest bronc rider forward or backwards

Rufus Green, Sr. (1923-1982)
Champion Calf Roper & Top Horse Trainer

Rufus Green, Sr., possessed a unique ability to communicate with horses. He became one of the best roping, hazing, barrel and cutting horse trainers of his time. Green Sr. began to enter local rodeos in South Texas to supplement his income. He was one of the first black cowboys to receive a Professional Rodeo Cowboy Association Membership Card. He was so successful that he quit his ranch job and became a full-time calf roper in the 1950's. Green competed over 2,000 rodeos all over the United States. He won money, saddles, trophies and belt buckles. Green trained over 1,000 horses and over 100 young men and women to compete in rodeos and horse riding competitions. He promoted race relations and integration in Rodeo and Western Culture every where he went. His students, clients, and friends were of all cultures.

Rufus Green, Sr. outstanding cowboy and horse trainer

Herb Jeffries (1913-2014)
First Black Singing Cowboy Movie Hero

Herb Jeffries entertainer, movie star, songwriter, author and lead singer of the Duke Ellington Band, hardly sums up the life and times of this legend. Born in a Detroit ghetto to an Irish mother and a Sicilian father, Herb Jeffries is not African-American at all. Jeffries knew that his 4 1/2 octave range would be his ticket to success. At 19, he auditioned for a club owner to play in an all-black jazz band. When the man questioned Jeffries' racial make-up, he spontaneously capitalized on his dark Italian features and claimed he was "Creole." That split decision would stay with him the rest of his life. Under the stage name Herbert Jeffrey, he starred with an all black cast, and sang as well as performed his own stunts in a series of singing cowboy westerns in the late 1930's including: *"Harlem on the Prairie,"* (1937) *"Two-Gun Man from Harlem,"* (1938) *"Harlem Rides the Range,"* (1939) and *"The Bronze Buckaroo,"* (1939), where his character *"Bob Blake"* rode a white horse named *"Star Dusk."* He became America's first black singing movie hero and provided encouragement and hope to children and adults of color during the early days of film.

Herb Jeffries movie star, lead singer and vintage renaissance man

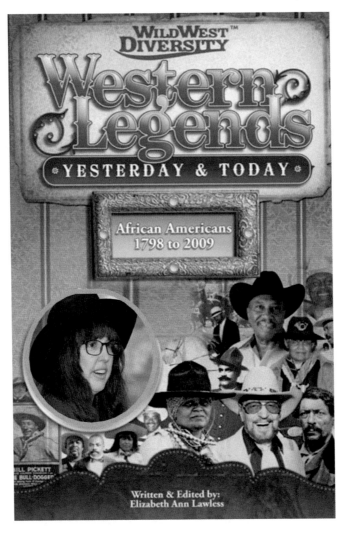

**FOR THE FULL STORIES CHECK OUT THE ORIGINAL BOOK
ESPECIALLY FOR MIDDLE SCHOOL AND ADULTS
AVAILABLE AT AMAZON, BARNES & NOBLE AND YOUR
LOCAL RETAIL OUTLETS.**

ELIZABETH ANN LAWLESS
AUTHOR & HOST WILD WEST DIVERSITY
LIVESTREAM, PODCAST & ENEWSLETTER

Liz is a 2x Amazon Best-Selling author, publisher, serial entrepreneur, speaker and host of Author Adventure and Wild West Diversity Livestreams, Podcasts and eNewsletters. In 1988, after 47 rejections from traditional publishers, she put her dream of book publishing away and jumped feet first into entrepreneurship. A question from a client in 1992 resurrected her publishing dream and today she is the author of 13 books which she self-published. In 2013, a request from a friend caused her to shift her business focus to helping others tell their compelling stories. Today Liz serves as a Book Catalyst with 110 Straight #1 Amazon Best-Sellers for clients and the Lead Creative for Wild West Diversity telling the rarely and untold stories of multicultural contributions to the settling of the American Wild West. You can follow her on social media @lawlessliz, @wildwestdiversity or @authorlizlawless or visit her websites at www.LizLawless.com or www.WildWestDiversity.com.

Made in the USA
Monee, IL
19 January 2024

51275769R10029